Love Please!

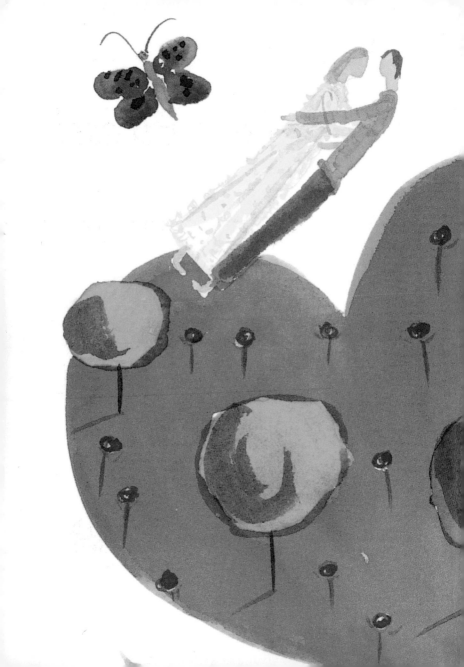

Love Please!

One Hundred
Passionate Poems

Edited by
A. D. P. Briggs

Illustrated by
Suzanna Hubbard

PHOENIX

A PHOENIX PAPERBACK

First published in Great Britain in 2001 by Phoenix,
an imprint of Orion Books Ltd,
Orion House, 5 Upper St Martin's Lane, London WC2H 9EA

A CIP catalogue record for this book
is available from the British Library.

ISBN 0 75381 121 9

Printed and bound in Italy.

Publisher's Note: A substantial amount of the material
in this book has already appeared under the title
Into a Towering Passion: Poems on Love.

~ Contents

~ Introduction

Love is a circle that doth move
In the same sweet eternity of love   ROBERT HERRICK

A Glory Circling Round the Soul

This grand phrase of Byron's ('Love') may sound excessive as a description of love, but its extravagance is understandable. Love is the biggest of all human subjects. Our lives are tiny, death is intractable and God seems far away. Of all the great ideas that dominate our existence only Love can be embraced as immediate and understandable as well as being elemental and eternal. There is nothing more important in a human life.

Love takes many forms, but for the purpose of this small collection we are considering Eros rather than Agape, amorous sexual relations rather than selfless devotion to other people. Behind Eros lies Biology. The reproduction of our species being our primary function, we animals need to bring male and female together with some urgency and frequency so that they can do what is necessary to get fertilised eggs implanted in wombs and new human beings on the way. But this is sexual attraction, not love. Why do we need love? Again, it is a matter of biology. Our astonishingly powerful brains, each containing as many neurons as there are stars in the Milky Way, need a long period for careful development, before and after birth. The human child, busily accommodating vast amounts of information and above all learning language, needs parental protection over several years before it can stand alone in the world. With this in mind, natural selection has favoured the creation of a strong bond between parents, thus increasing the chances of their mutual devotion over the necessary span. That invisible bond is love, and it holds human affairs together like gravity binding the universe.

The Secret of the Sun

Love as a literary subject is massive and complex. At its most lurid the force is seen by the poets as something of transcendant power, sometimes as mighty as the universe itself. Robert Bridges views our world as a creation of love, and love itself as the unique means of understanding the universe in macro- and microcosm:

> Love can tell, and love alone,
> Whence the million stars were strewn,
> Why each atom knows its own...
> ('My delight and thy delight')

Earlier he has claimed that 'Love ... Hath the secret of the sun', all of which seems like a genuine attempt to relate humanity to the cosmos through poetry. This is not usually the case. More commonly a poet, smitten by the full force of love, will be so fired with enthusiasm that only hyperbole will suffice to express such powerful feelings. Thus Robbie Burns will profess himself capable of loving 'till a' the seas gang dry' and 'the rocks melt wi' the sun' ('A Red, Red Rose'). Elizabeth Barrett Browning (translating from the Portuguese) loves 'to the depth and breadth and height/ [Her] soul can reach, when feeling out of sight/For the ends of Being…' ('How do I love thee? Let me count the ways'); and Robert Southey describes his love, which descends from heaven and shall return there, as 'indestructible' ('Love Cannot Die').

The mention of heaven is instructive. If not the cosmos, then divinity is frequently invoked as the only metaphor large enough to convey the truth of love. Byron describes it as 'A feeling from the Godhead caught' ('Love'); Campion compares his mistress's face to a heavenly paradise and her eyes to watching angels ('There is a garden in her face'); Hopkins, inviting God to a wedding, sees the lovers as bound to each other by divine charity 'déeper than divined' ('At the Wedding March'); Thomas D'Urfey, while insisting on Chloe's physicality, still compares her to a saint and a goddess and calls her divine in the last word of his poem ('Chloe Divine'). For good measure, though, we should note that two and a half centuries ago William Cartwright dismissed this sort of thing as 'thin love' and called back down to earth those 'that tread Those vain aerial ways' with a reminder that love dwells in the body more than the spirit ('No Platonic Love').

The Cruel Madness of Love

The course of love cannot be expected ever to run smooth. It causes as much anguish as delight. Tennyson despaired of it, putting these sardonic words into the mouth of the narrator of *Maud*:

> And most of all would I flee from the cruel madness of love,
> The honey of poison-flowers and all the measureless ill.

For every joyous love poem there is one of agony. Love is a

sickness, torment and tempest ('Love is a sickness…'), a bleeding wound ('Red and White Roses'), sweetness turned to bitterness ('Grown and Flown'), a painful, unspoken secret ('I hid my love…'), an affliction worse than blindness ('Cards and Kisses'), a smarting pain that can be assuaged only by sleep or death. It is irrational ('Love's Logic) and chancy ('And if I did what then?'). It is elusive and complicated, infuriating and uncontrollable. Worst of all, once attained it is likely to dissolve rapidly and disappear. At least a quarter of the poems in this book will complain that love is too short-lived to provide lasting satisfaction. Why should this be so?

For one thing, death used to intervene between lovers when they were still young, removing one of them prematurely. Many sad phrases adorn the following pages, marking the early passing of a loved one. But all too often it is not the lover, but love itself, that dies. George Meredith explains why: love can never last because of human frailty

> Here is a fitting spot to dig Love's grave…
> We are betray'd by what is false within.
> ('Love's Grave')

The very darkest side of love, nothing less than evil lust, is depicted in an extract from Lord Macaulay's 'Virginia (Lays of Ancient Rome)'. Lucrece is a pretty young girl observed by Appius as she trips home from school; it is painfully certain that all will end in tragedy when we read

> And all along the Forum, and up the Sacred Street,
> His vulture eye pursued the trip of those small glancing feet.

This unpleasant extract from a narrative poem puts into cold perspective the many flippant comments on infidelity dashed off by the other casual lovers, but – thank heaven – there is no suggestion in this collection or in the entire run of English lyric poetry that brutal violence belongs anywhere near the norm of erotic experience.

The Lineaments of Gratified Desire

These thoughts bring us to the subject of sex, which underlies all questions of love. It is only the degree of frankness that varies. William Blake was remarkably forthright on this subject in 'The Question Answered'. What do men require from women? The same thing that women require from men – sexual satisfaction, 'the lineaments of gratified desire'. Many other poets have spoken along similar lines. William Cartwright, speaking of finding 'med'cine for the itch', reminds us that when lovers come together soul by soul 'the body is the way'. For him the process is inescapable. Whenever I have climbed from sex to soul, and from soul to thought, he recalls, 'From soul I lighted at the sex agen'. Hence the title of his poem in the mid-seventeenth century, 'No Platonic Love'. The woman's point of view is put by Thomas Parnell, the singer of whose 'Song' wants the best of both worlds. She will continue to appear like an angel, 'But still be a woman to you.' The most thrilling line in this poem is the highly sensual

When your love runs in blushes throughout every vein…

Sometimes the poet has to be discreet while wanting to purvey the same message. Robert Herrick's famous description of Julia's attire, with its unforgettable reference to 'The liquefaction of her clothes' ('Upon Julia's Clothes'), is, of course, really addressed to the lovely body within that causes them to flow so sweetly. A splendid example of overt sexual parallelism is found in John Fletcher's 'My Man Thomas'. (Put together the names John and Thomas and you have the subject in hand.) Most of the dialogue in this brief poem comes from the girl who has invited Thomas to visit her at night; he announces his arrival and she welcomes him, indicating where he is to be 'lodged' and using the word 'come' five times in a ten-word span. Nothing indecent here, of course, though the full meaning of the encounter is unmistakable. Another way of dealing with sexual arousal in a decorous manner is to say what did not happen between the lovers, however narrowly they may have skirted disaster. Thomas Moore's poignantly named 'Did Not' brings lips and bodies into close erotic proximity, raises the temperature unbearably, yet still leaves us with

> ... lovers, who so nearly erred,
> And yet, who did not.

Seldom can so much have been said in negative terms about the raging reality of physical passion.

Of course there are some writers, well before the twentieth century, who throw caution to the winds in these matters and call spades spades. The anonymous writer of an early fifteenth-century poem laughs at allegory when he begins with the words, 'I have a gentil cock...' and ends by telling us that 'every night he percheth him in my lady's chamber.' But John Wilmot, Earl of Rochester, takes the prize as the most outspoken English poet on sexual performances of every kind. In this collection we have included his wonderful little hymn, 'A Song of a Young Lady to Her Ancient Lover'. She describes what she will do to restore his 'youthful heat'. It will involve taking hold of

> The nobler part, which but to name
> In our sex would be counted shame.

Her reviving hand will soon ensure that this organ shall 'In former warmth and vigour stand'. No place here for embarrassment or prudery.

Only slightly less explicit is William Shakespeare in an extract from his first publication, a tragic narrative poem of 1589, 'Venus and Adonis'. Venus offers her all to an unresponsive lover:

> I'll be a Park, and thou shalt be my Deer.
> Feed where thou wilt, on Mountain or in Dale;
>> Graze on my Lips, and if those Hills be dry
>> Stray lower, where the pleasant Fountains lie.

This seldom-read poem, which is much too long for its own good, contains much erotic material of this kind.

Our last example of overt sexuality in poetry comes from John Donne ('Going to Bed'). It is worth waiting for. Urging his lover to prepare for bed, the poet instructs her in the art of undressing, finds the normal response in himself and finally pleads with her to let him start the love-making.

> License my roving hands, and let them go,
> Before, behind, between, above, below.
> Oh my America! My new-found-land…

Here is a clever little piece of literature. Surely love-making demands the use of caressing adjectives, dynamic verbs, and lofty conceits. What shall the ignoble and uninteresting *preposition* do in this company? Here is its moment of greatest glory. The second of these lines, which might claim to be one of the most erotically-charged in the English language, consists of improbable ingredients – five prepositions, each one disyllabic and alliterative, mockingly confident and full of the good humour that should never be far away from love itself.

From all the riches of English love poetry we have chosen one hundred works, each by a different poet. For the sake of variety, they have been placed not chronologically but in alphabetical order according to the name of the poet.

A. D. P. BRIGGS

Love Please!

An Evening

A sunset's mounded cloud;
   A diamond evening-star;
   Sad blue hills afar;
     Love in his shroud.

Scarcely a tear to shed;
   Hardly a word to say;
   The end of a summer day;
     Sweet Love dead.

'I have a gentil cock...'

I have a gentil cock, croweth me day
he doth me risen early, my matins for to say

I have a gentil cock, comen he is of great
his comb is of red coral, his tail is of jet

I have a gentil cock, comen he is of kind
his comb is of red sorrel, his tail is of inde

his legs be of azure, so gentil and so small
his spurs are of silver white, into the wortewale

his eyes are of crystal, locked all in amber
and every night he percheth him in my lady's chamber

Love's Logic

I HER RESPECTABLE PAPA'S

'My dear, be sensible! Upon my word
This – for a woman even – is absurd;
His income's not a hundred pounds, I know;
He's not worth loving.' – 'But I love him so!'

II HER MOTHER'S

'You silly child! He is well made and tall;
But looks are far from being all in all.
His social standing's low, his family's low;
He's not worth loving.' – 'And I love him so!'

III HER ETERNAL FRIEND'S

'Is that he picking up the fallen fan?
My dear, he's such an awkward, ugly man!
You must be certain, pet, to answer "No".
He's not worth loving.' – 'And I love him so!'

IV HER BROTHER'S

'By Jove! were I a girl – through horrid hap -
I wouldn't have a milk-and-water chap.
The man has not a single spark of "go";
He's not worth loving.' – 'Yet I love him so!'

V HER OWN

'And were he everything to which I've listened;
Though he were ugly, awkward (and he isn't),
Poor, low-born, and destitute of "go",
He is worth loving, for I love him so!'

Absence

In this fair stranger's eyes of grey
Thine eyes, my love! I see.
I shiver; for the passing day
Had borne me far from thee.

This is the curse of life! that not
A nobler, calmer train
Of wiser thoughts and feelings blot
Our passions from our brain;

But each day brings its petty dust
Our soon-choked souls to fill,
And we forget because we must
And not because we will.

I struggle towards the light; and ye
Once-long'd-for storms of love!
If with the light ye cannot be,
I bear that ye remove.

I struggle towards the light – but oh
While yet the night is chill,
Upon time's barren, stormy flow,
Stay with me, Marguerite, still!

In a Bath Teashop

'Let us not speak, for the love we bear one another –
    Let us hold hands and look.'
She, such a very ordinary little woman;
    He, such a thumping crook:
But both, for the moment, little lower than the angels
    In the teashop inglenook.

The Question Answered

What is it men in women do require?
The lineaments of gratified desire.
What is it women do in men require?
The lineaments of gratified desire.

'The night has a thousand eyes'

The night has a thousand eyes,
   And the day but one;
Yet the light of the bright world dies
   With the dying sun.

The mind has a thousand eyes,
   And the heart but one;
Yet the light of a whole life dies
   When love is done.

'My delight and thy delight'

My delight and thy delight
Walking, like two angels white,
In the gardens of the night:

My desire and thy desire
Twining to a tongue of fire,
Leaping live, and laughing higher:

Thro' the everlasting strife
In the mystery of life.
Love, from whom the world begun,
Hath the secret of the sun.

Love can tell, and love alone,
Whence the million stars were strewn,
Why each atom knows its own,
How, in spite of woe and death,
Gay is life, and sweet is breath:

This he taught us, this we knew,
Happy in his science true,
Hand in hand as we stood
'Neath the shadows of the wood,
Heart to heart as we lay
In the dawning of the day.

Love and Friendship

Love is like the wild rose-briar,
Friendship like the holly-tree –
The holly is dark when the rose-briar blooms
But which will bloom most constantly?

The wild rose-briar is sweet in spring,
Its summer blossoms scent the air;
Yet wait till winter comes again,
And who will call the wild-briar fair?

Then, scorn the silly rose-wreath now
And deck thee with the holly's sheen,
That when December blights thy brow
He still may leave thy garland green.

Meeting at Night

The grey sea and the long black land;
And the yellow half-moon large and low;
And the startled little waves that leap
In fiery ringlets from their sleep,
As I gain the cove with pushing prow,
And quench its speed i' the slushy sand.

Then a mile of warm sea-scented beach;
Three fields to cross till a farm appears;
A tap at the pane, the quick sharp scratch
And blue spurt of a lighted match,
And a voice less loud, thro' its joys and fears,
Than the two hearts beating each to each!

'She bewitched me'

She bewitched me
With such a sweet and genial charm,
I knew not when I wounded was,
And when I found it, hugged the harm.

Down hill; ah yes – down hill, down hill I glide,
But such a hill!
One tapestried fall of meadow pride,
Of ladysmock and daffodil.

How soon, how soon adown a rocky stair,
And slips no longer smooth as they are sweet,
Shall I, with backward-streaming hair,
Outfly my bleeding feet?

A Red, Red Rose

O my Luve's like a red, red rose,
That's newly sprung in June;
O my Luve's like the melodie
That's sweetly play'd in tune.

As fair art thou, my bonnie lass,
So deep in luve am I:
And I will love thee still, my Dear,
Till a' the seas gang dry.

Till a' the seas gang dry, my Dear,
And the rocks melt wi' the sun;
I will love thee still, my Dear,
While the sands o' life shall run.

And fare thee weel, my only Luve,
And fare thee weel, a while!
And I will come again, my Luve,
Tho' it were ten thousand mile!

Love

Yes, Love indeed is light from heaven;
    A spark of that immortal fire
With angels shared, by Alla given,
    To lift from earth our low desire.
Devotion wafts the mind above,
But heaven itself descends in love;
A feeling from the Godhead caught,
To wean from self each sordid thought;
A ray of Him who formed the whole;
A glory circling round the soul!

Freedom and Love

How delicious is the winning
Of a kiss at Love's beginning,
When two mutual hearts are sighing
For the knot there's no untying!

Yet remember, 'midst our wooing
Love has bliss, but Love has ruing;
Other smiles may make you fickle,
Tears for other charms may trickle.

Love he comes, and Love he tarries,
Just as fate our fancy carries;
Longest stays, when sorest chidden;
Laughs and flies, when press'd and bidden.

Bind the sea to slumber stilly,
Bind its odour to the lily,
Bind the aspen ne'er to quiver,
Then bind Love to last forever.

Love's a fire that needs renewal
Of fresh beauty for its fuel:
Love's wing moults when caged and captured,
Only free, he soars enraptured.

Can you keep the bee from ranging
Or the ringdove's neck from changing?
No! nor fetter'd Love from dying
In the knot there's no untying.

'There is a garden in her face'

There is a garden in her face,
Where roses and white lilies grow;
A heavenly paradise is that place,
Wherein all pleasant fruits do grow;
There cherries grow that none may buy
Till 'cherry ripe' themselves do cry.

Those cherries fairly do enclose
Of orient pearl a double row,
Which, when her lovely laughter shows,
They look like rosebuds fill'd with snow;
Yet them no peer nor prince may buy
Till 'cherry ripe' themselves do cry.

Her eyes like angels watch them still,
Her brows like bended bows do stand,
Threatening with piercing frowns to kill
All that approach with eye or hand
These sacred cherries to come nigh,
Till 'cherry ripe' themselves do cry.

Red and White Roses

Read in these Roses the sad story
Of my hard fate, and your owne glory.
In the White you may discover
The paleness of a fainting lover;
In the Red the flames still feeding
On my heart, with fresh wounds bleeding.
The White will tell you how I languish,
And the Red express my anguish;
The White my innocence displaying,
The Red my martyrdom betraying.
The frowns that on your brow resided,
Have those Roses thus divided.
Oh! let your smiles but clear the weather,
And then they both shall grow together.

No Platonic Love

Tell me no more of minds embracing minds,
And hearts exchang'd for hearts;
That spirits spirits meet, as winds do winds,
And mix their subt'lest parts;
That two unbodied essences may kiss,
And then like angels, twist and feel one bliss.

I was that silly thing that once was wrought
To practise this thin love;
I climb'd from sex to soul, from soul to thought;
But thinking there to move,
Headlong I roll'd from thought to soul, and then
From soul I lighted at the sex agen.

As some strict down-look'd men pretend to fast
Who yet in closets eat;
So lovers who profess they spirits taste,
Feed yet on grosser meat;
I know they boast they souls to souls convey,
Howe'er they meet, the body is the way.

Come, I will undeceive thee, they that tread
Those vain aerial ways,
Are like young heirs and alchymists misled
To waste their wealth and days,
For searching thus to be for ever rich,
They only find a med'cine for the itch.

To Rosamounde
A Balade

Madame, ye ben of al beauté shryne
As fer as cercled is the mapemounde,
For as the cristal glorious ye shyne,
And lyke ruby ben your chekes rounde.
Therwith ye ben so mery and so jocounde
That at a revel whan that I see you daunce,
It is an oynement unto my wounde,
Thogh ye to me ne do no daliaunce.

For thogh I wepe of teres ful a tyne,
Yet may that wo myn herte nat confounde;
Your seemly voys, that ye so smal outtwyne,
Maketh my thoght in joye and blis habounde.
So curtaysly I go, with love bounde,
That to myself I sey, in my penaunce,
'Suffyseth me to love you, Rosamounde,
Thogh ye to me ne do no daliaunce.'

Nas never pyk walwed in galauntyne
As I in love am walwed and ywounde,
For which ful ofte I of myself devyne
That I am trewe Tristam the secounde.
My love may not refreyd be nor affounde;
I brenne ay in an amorous plesaunce.
Do what you lyst, I wil your thral be founde,
Thogh ye to me ne do no daliaunce.

'I hid my love...'

I hid my love when young till I
Couldn't bear the buzzing of a fly;
I hid my love to my despite
Till I could not bear to look at light:
I dare not gaze upon her face
But left her memory in each place;
Where'er I saw a wild flower lie
I kissed and bade my love good-bye.

I met her in the greenest dells,
Where dewdrops pearl the wood bluebells;
The lost breeze kissed her bright blue eye,
The bee kissed and went singing by,
A sunbeam found a passage there,
A gold chain round her neck so fair;
As secret as the wild bee's song
She lay there all the summer long.

I hid my love in field and town
Till e'en the breeze would knock me down;
The bees seemed singing ballads o'er,
The fly's bass turned a lion's roar;
And even silence found a tongue,
To haunt me all the summer long;
The riddle nature could not prove
Was nothing else but secret love.

Jealousy

'The myrtle bush grew shady
   Down by the ford.' –
'Is it even so?' said my lady.
   'Even so!' said my lord.
'The leaves are set too thick together
   For the point of a sword.'

'The arras in your room hangs close,
   No light between!
You wedded one of those
   That see unseen.' –
'Is it even so?' said the King's Majesty.
   'Even so!' said the Queen.

Answer to a Child's Question

Do you ask what the birds say? The Sparrow, the Dove,
The Linnet and Thrush say, 'I love and I love!'
In the winter they're silent – the wind is so strong;
What it says, I don't know, but it sings a loud song.
But green leaves, and blossoms, and sunny warm weather,
And singing, and loving – all come back together.

But the Lark is so brimful of gladness and love,
The green fields below him, the blue sky above,
That he sings, and he sings; and for ever sings he -
'I love my Love, and my Love loves me!'

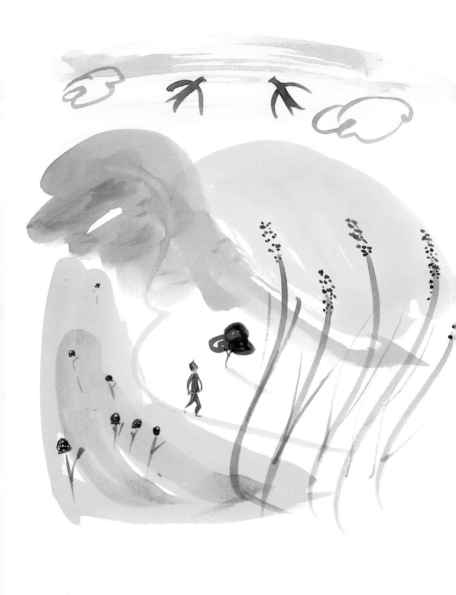

Song

Pious Selinda goes to prayers,
    If I but ask the favour;
And yet the tender fool's in tears,
    When she believes I'll leave her.

Would I were free from this restraint,
    Or else had hopes to win her;
Would she could make of me a saint,
    Or I of her a sinner.

'i like my body...'

i like my body when it is with your
body. It is so quite new a thing.
Muscles better and nerves more.
i like your body. i like what it does,
i like its hows. i like to feel the spine
of your body and its bones, and the trembling
-firm-smooth ness and which i will
again and again and again
kiss, i like kissing this and that of you,
i like, slowly stroking the, shocking fuzz
of your electric fur, and what-is-it comes
over parting flesh .... And eyes big love-crumbs,

and possibly i like the thrill

of under me you so quite new

'Love is a sickness...'

Love is a sickness full of woes,
   All remedies refusing;
A plant that with most cutting grows,
   Most barren with best using.
           Why so?
More we enjoy it, more it dies;
If not enjoy'd, it sighing cries –
           Heigh ho!

Love is a torment of the mind,
   A tempest everlasting;
And Jove hath made it of a kind
   Not well, nor full nor fasting.
           Why so?
More we enjoy it, more it dies;
If not enjoy'd, it sighing cries –
           Heigh ho!

'Under the willow-shades...'

Under the willow-shades they were
   Free from the eye-sight of the sun,
For no intruding beam could there
   Peep through to spy what things were done:
     Thus sheltered they unseen did lie,
     Surfeiting on each other's eye;
Defended by the willow-shades alone,
The sun's heat they defied and cooled their own.

Whilst they did embrace unspied,
   The conscious willow seemed to smile,
That them with privacy supplied,
   Holding the door, as 't were, the while;
     And when their dalliances were o'er,
     The willows, to oblige them more,
Bowing, did seem to say, as they withdrew,
'We can supply you with a cradle too.'

'My life closed twice before its close'

My life closed twice before its close;
   It yet remains to see
If Immortality unveil
   A third event to me

So huge, so hopeless to conceive,
   As these that twice befell.
Parting is all we know of heaven,
   And all we need of hell.

Urceus Exit: Triolet

I intended an Ode,
   And it turn'd to a Sonnet
It began *à la mode,*
I intended an Ode;
But Rose cross'd the road
   In her latest new bonnet;
I intended an Ode;
   And it turn'd to a Sonnet.

Going to Bed

Come, Madam, come, all rest my powers defy,
Until I labour, I in labour lie.
The foe oft-times having the foe in sight
Is tired with standing though he never fight.
Off with that girdle, like heaven's zone glittering,
But a far fairer world incompassing.
Unpin that spangled breastplate which you wear,
That th'eyes of busy fools may be stopt there.
Unlace yourself, for that harmonious chime
Tells me from you that now it is bed time.
Off with that happy busk, which I envie,
That still can be, and still can stand so nigh.
Your gown going off such beauteous state reveals
As when from flow'ry meads th'hill's shadow steals.
Off with that wiry coronet and show
The hairy diadem which on you doth grow:
Now off with those shoes, and then safely tread
In this love's hallow'd temple, this soft bed.
In such white robes, heaven's angels us'd to be
Receiv'd by men: thou angel bring'st with thee
A heaven like Mahomet's paradise; and though
Ill spirits walk in white, we easily know
By this these angels from an evil sprite,
Those set our hairs, but these our flesh upright.
   License my roving hands, and let them go,
Before, behind, between, above, below.

O my America! my new-found-land,
My kingdom, safeliest when with one man mann'd,
My mine of precious stones, my emperie,
How blest am I in this discovering thee!
To enter in these bonds, is to be free;
Then where my hand is set, my seal shall be.

    Full nakedness! All joys are due to thee,
As souls unbodied, bodies uncloth'd must be,
To taste whole joys. Gems which you women use
Are like Atlanta's balls, cast in men's views,
That when a fool's eye lighteth on a gem,
His earthly soul may covet theirs, not them.
Like pictures, or like books' gay coverings made
For lay-men, are all women thus array'd;
Themselves are mystic books, which only we
(Whom their imputed grace will dignify)
Must see reveal'd. Then since that I may know,
As liberally, as to a midwife, show
Thy self: cast all, yea, this white linen hence,
There is no penance due to innocence.

    To teach thee, I am naked first; why then
What need'st thou have more covering than a man?

Non Sum Qualis Eram Bonae Sub Regno Cynarae

Last night, ah, yesternight, betwixt her lips and mine
There fell thy shadow, Cynara! thy breath was shed
Upon my soul between the kisses and the wine;
And I was desolate and sick of an old passion,
    Yea, I was desolate and bow'd my head:
I have been faithful to thee, Cynara! in my fashion.

All night upon mine heart I felt her warm heart beat,
Night-long within mine arms in love and sleep she lay;
Surely the kisses of her bought red mouth were sweet;
But I was desolate and sick of an old passion,
    When I awoke and found the dawn was gray:
I have been faithful to thee, Cynara! in my fashion.

I have forgot much, Cynara! gone with the wind,
Flung roses, roses, riotously with the throng,
Dancing, to put thy pale lost lilies out of mind;
But I was desolate and sick of an old passion,
    Yea, all the time, because the dance was long:
I have been faithful to thee, Cynara! in my fashion.

I cried for madder music and for stronger wine,
But when the feast is finish'd and the lamps expire,
Then falls thy shadow, Cynara! the night is thine;
And I am desolate and sick of an old passion,
    Yea, hungry for the lips of my desire:
I have been faithful to thee, Cynara! in my fashion.

'Nothing but no and I, and I and no'

Nothing but no and I, and I and no,
How falls it out so strangely you reply?
I tell ye, fair, I'll not be answered so,
With this affirming no, denying I.
I say, I love, you sleightly answer, I:
I say, you love, you pule me out a no:
I say, I die, you echo me with I:
Save me, I cry, you sigh me out a no;

Must woe and I have nought but no and I?
No I am I, if I no more can have;
Answer no more, with silence make reply,
And let me take myself what I do crave,
    Let no and I, with I and you be so:
    Then answer no and I, and I and no.

'Ah, how sweet...'

Ah, how sweet it is to love,
Ah, how gay is young desire!
And what pleasing pains we prove
When we first approach Love's fire!
Pains of Love are sweeter far
Than all other pleasures are.

Sighs which are from Lovers blown
Do but gently heave the Heart:
Ev'n the tears they shed alone
Cure, like trickling Balm, their smart.
Lovers, when they lose their breath,
Bleed away in easie death.

Love and Time with reverence use,
Treat 'em like a parting friend:
Nor the golden gifts refuse
Which in youth sincere they send:
For each year their price is more,
And they less simple than before.

Love, like Spring-tides full and high,
Swells in every youthful vein:
But each Tide does less supply,
Till they quite shrink in again.
If a flow in Age appear,
'Tis but rain, and runs not clear.

Chloe Divine

Chloe's a Nymph in flowery groves,
    A Nereid in the streams;
Saint-like she in the temple moves,
    A woman in my dreams.

Love steals artillery from her eyes,
    The Graces point her charms;
Orpheus is rivall'd in her voice,
    And Venus in her arms.

Never so happily in one
    Did heaven and earth combine:
And yet 'tis flesh and blood alone
    That makes her so divine.

To a Lady Asking Him How Long He Would Love Her

It is not, Celia, in our power
　　To say how long our love will last;
It may be we within this hour
　　May lose those joys we now do taste;
The Blessèd, that immortal be,
From change in love are only free.

Then since we mortal lovers are,
　　Ask not how long our love will last;
But while it does, let us take care
　　Each minute be with pleasure past:
Were it not madness to deny
To live because we're sure to die?

'My man Thomas'

My man Thomas
Did me promise
He would visit me this night.

I am here, love;
Tell me, dear love,
How I may obtain thy sight.

Come up to my window, love;
Come, come, come:
Come to my window, my dear;
The wind nor the rain
Shall trouble thee again,
But thou shalt be lodged here.

'Oh no more, no more, too late'

Oh no more, no more, too late
Sighs are spent; the burning tapers
Of a life as chaste as Fate,
Pure as are unwritten papers,
    Are burnt out: no heat, no light
    Now remains, 'tis ever night.
Love is dead, let lovers' eyes,
    Lock'd in endless dreams,
    Th'extreme of all extremes,
Ope no more, for now Love dies,
    Now Love dies, implying
Love's martyrs must be ever, ever dying.

'And if I did what then?'

And if I did what then?
Are you aggriev'd therefore?
The sea hath fish for every man,
And what would you have more?

Thus did my Mistress once,
Amaze my mind with doubt:
And popt a question for the nonce,
To beat my brains about.

Whereto I thus replied,
Each fisherman can wish,
That all the sea at every ride,
Were his alone to fish.

And so did I (in vain),
But since it may not be:
Let such fish there as find the gain,
And leave the loss for me.

And with such luck and loss,
I will content my self:
Till tides of turning time may toss,
Such fishers on the shelf.

And when they stick on sands,
That every man may see:
Then will I laugh and clap my hands,
As they do now at me.

Song

When lovely woman stoops to folly,
   And finds too late that men betray,
What charm can soothe her melancholy;
   What art can wash her guilt away?

The only art her guilt to cover,
   To hide her shame from every eye,
To give repentance to her lover,
   And wring his bosom – is to die.

Down, Wanton, Down!

Down, wanton, down! Have you no shame
That at the whisper of Love's name,
Or Beauty's, presto! up you raise
Your angry head and stand at gaze?

Poor bombard-captain, sworn to reach
The ravelin and effect a breach –
Indifferent what you storm or why,
So be that in the breach you die!

Love may be blind, but Love at least
Knows what is man and what mere beast;
Or Beauty wayward, but requires
More delicacy from her squires.

Tell me, my witless, whose one boast
Could be your staunchness at the post,
When were you made a man of parts
To think fine and profess the arts?

Will many-gifted Beauty come
Bowing to your bald rule of thumb,
Or Love swear loyalty to your crown?
Be gone, have done! Down, wanton, down!

The Voice

Woman much missed, how you call to me, call to me,
Saying that now you are not as you were
When you had changed from the one who was all to me,
But as at first, when our day was fair.

Can it be you that I hear? Let me view you, then,
Standing as when I drew near to the town
Where you would wait for me: yes, as I knew you then,
Even to the original air-blue gown!

Or is it only the breeze, in its listlessness
Travelling across the wet mead to me here,
You being ever consigned to existlessness,
    Heard no more again far or near?

    Thus I: faltering forward,
    Leaves around me falling,
Wind oozing thin through the thorn from norward,
    And the woman calling.

What the Bullet Sang

O joy of creation,
       To be!
O rapture, to fly
       And be free!
Be the battle lost or won,
Though its smoke shall hide the sun,
I shall find my love – the one
       Born for me!

I shall know him where he stands
       All alone,
With the power in his hands
       Not o'erthrown;
I shall know him by his face,
By his godlike front and grace;
I shall hold him for a space
       All my own!

It is he – O my love!
       So bold!
It is I – all thy love
       Foretold!
It is I – O love, what bliss!
Dost thou answer to my kiss?
O sweetheart! what is this
       Lieth there so cold?

A Dream of Jealousy

Walking with you and another lady
In wooded parkland, the whispering grass
Ran its fingers through our guessing silence
And the trees opened into a shady
Unexpected clearing where we sat down.
I think the candour of the light dismayed us.
We talked about desire and being jealous,
Our conversation a loose single gown
Or a white picnic tablecloth spread out
Like a book of manners in the wilderness.
'Show me,' I said to our companion, 'what
I have much coveted, your breast's mauve star.'
And she consented. O neither these verses
Nor my prudence, love, can heal your wounded stare.

Love

Love bade me welcome; yet my soul drew back,
      Guilty of dust and sin.
But quick-eyed Love, observing me grow slack
      From my first entrance in,
Drew nearer to me, sweetly questioning,
      If I lack anything.

'A guest,' I answered, 'worthy to be here.'
      Love said, 'You shall be he.'
'I, the unkind, ungrateful! Ah, my dear,
      I cannot look on Thee.'
Love took my hand, and smiling, did reply,
      'Who made the eyes but I?'

'Truth, Lord, but I have marred them; let my shame
      Go where it doth deserve.'
'And know you not,' said Love, 'who bore the blame?'
      'My dear, then I will serve.'
'You must sit down,' said Love, 'and taste my meat.'
      So I did sit and eat.

Upon Julia's Clothes

Whenas in silks my Julia goes,
Then, then, methinks, how sweetly flows
The liquefaction of her clothes.

Next, when I cast mine eyes and see
That brave vibration each way free,
O how that glittering taketh me!

Ruth

Love, see thy lover humbled at thy feet,
Not in servility, but homage sweet,
Gladly inclined: – and with my bended knee
Think that my inward spirit bows to thee -
More proud indeed than when I stand or climb
Elsewhere: – there is no statue so sublime
As Love's in all the world, and e'en to kiss
The pedestal is still a better bliss
Than all ambitions. O! Love's lowest base
Is far above the reaching of disgrace
To shame this posture. Let me then draw nigh
Feet that have fared so nearly to the sky,
And when this duteous homage has been given
I will rise up and clasp the heart in Heaven.

At the Wedding March

God with honour hang your head,
Groom, and grace you, bride, your bed
With lissome scions, sweet scions,
Out of hallowed bodies bred.

Each be other's comfort kind:
Déep, déeper than divined,
Divine charity, dear charity,
Fast you ever, fast bind.

Then let the march tread our ears:
I to him turn with tears
Who to wedlock, his wonder wedlock,
Déals tríumph and immortal years.

'When I was one-and-twenty'

When I was one-and-twenty
    I heard a wise man say,
'Give crowns and pounds and guineas
    But not your heart away;
Give pearls away and rubies
    But keep your fancy free.'
But I was one-and-twenty,
    No use to talk to me.

When I was one-and-twenty
    I heard him say again,
'The heart out of the bosom
    Was never given in vain;
'Tis paid with sighs a plenty
    And sold for endless rue.'
And I am two-and-twenty,
    And oh, 'tis true, 'tis true.

'Jenny kiss'd me...'

Jenny kiss'd me when we met,
    Jumping from the chair she sat in;
Time, you thief, who love to get
    Sweets into your list, put that in!
Say I'm weary, say I'm sad,
    Say that health and wealth have miss'd me,
Say I'm growing old, but add,
    Jenny kiss'd me.

To Celia

Drink to me only with thine eyes,
And I will pledge with mine;
Or leave a kiss but in the cup
And I'll not look for wine.
The thirst that from the soul doth rise
Doth ask a drink divine;
But might I of Jove's nectar sup
I would not change for thine.

I sent thee late a rosy wreath,
Not so much honouring thee
As giving it a hope, that there
It could not wither'd be;
But thou thereon did'st only breathe
And sent'st it back to me;
Since when it grows, and smells, I swear,
Not of itself, but thee.

The Eve of St Agnes

(Extract)

And still she slept an azure-lidded sleep,
In blanched linen, smooth, and lavendered,
While he from forth the closet brought a heap
Of candied apple, quince, and plum, and gourd;
With jellies soother than the creamy curd,
And lucent syrops, tinct with cinnamon;
Manna and dates, in argosy transferred
From Fez; and spiced dainties, every one,
From silken Samarcand to cedared Lebanon.

These delicates he heaped with glowing hand
On golden dishes and in baskets bright
Of wreathed silver: sumptuous they stand
In the retired quiet of the night,
Filling the chilly room with perfume light. –
'And now, my love, my seraph fair, awake!
Thou art my heaven, and I thine eremite:
Open thine eyes, for meek St Agnes' sake,
Or I shall drowse beside thee, so my soul doth ache.'

Thus whispering, his warm, unnerved arm
Sank in her pillow. Shaded was her dream
By the dusk curtains: — 'twas a midnight charm
Impossible to melt as iced stream:
The lustrous salvers in the moonlight gleam;
Broad golden fringe upon the carpet lies:
It seemed he never, never could redeem
From such a stedfast spell his lady's eyes
So mused awhile, entoiled in woofed phantasies.

'Proud word you never spoke...'

Proud word you never spoke, but you will speak
   Four not exempt from pride some future day.
Resting on one white hand a warm wet cheek
   Over my open volume you will say,
    'This man loved *me*!' then rise and trip away.

Annus Mirabilis

Sexual intercourse began
In nineteen sixty-three
(Which was rather late for me) –
Between the end of the *Chatterley* ban
And the Beatles' first LP.

Up till then there'd only been
A sort of bargaining,
A wrangle for a ring,
A shame that started at sixteen
And spread to everything.

Then all at once the quarrel sank:
Everyone felt the same,
And every life became
A brilliant breaking of the bank,
A quite unlosable game.

So life was never better than
In nineteen sixty-three
(Though just too late for me) –
Between the end of the *Chatterley* ban
And the Beatles' first LP.

Hiawatha's Wooing (Hiawatha)

(Extract)

Yes, as in a dream she listened
To the words of Hiawatha,
As he talked of old Nokomis,
Who had nursed him in his childhood,
As he told of his companions,
Chibiabos, the musician,
And the very strong man, Kwasind,
And of happiness and plenty
In the land of the Ojibways,
In the pleasant land and peaceful.
'After many years of warfare,
Many years of strife and bloodshed,
There is peace between the Ojibways
And the tribe of the Dacotahs.'
Thus continued Hiawatha,
And then added, speaking slowly,
'That this peace may last for ever,
And our hands be clasped more closely,
And our hearts be more united,
Give me as my wife this maiden,
Minnehaha, Laughing Water,
Loveliest of Dacotah women!'
And the ancient Arrow-maker
Paused a moment ere he answered,
Smoked a little while in silence,

Looked at Hiawatha proudly,
Fondly looked at Laughing Water,
And made answer, very gravely:
'Yes, if Minnehaha wishes;
Let your heart speak, Minnehaha!'
    And the lovely Laughing Water
Seemed more lovely, as she stood there
Neither willing nor reluctant,
As she went to Hiawatha,
Softly took the seat beside him,
While she said, and blushed to say it,
'I will follow you, my husband!'
    This was Hiawatha's wooing!

To Althea From Prison

When love with unconfinèd wings
   Hovers within my gates,
And my divine Althea brings
   To whisper at my grates;
When I lie tangled in her hair,
   And fettered to her eye,
The birds that wanton in the air
   Know no such liberty.

When flowing cups run swiftly round,
   With no allaying Thames –
Our careless heads with roses bound,
   Our hearts with loyal flames;
When thirsty grief in wine we steep;
   When healths and draughts go free,
Fishes that tipple in the deep
   Know no such liberty.

When, linnet-like confinèd, I
   With shriller throat shall sing
The sweetness, mercy, majesty,
   And glories of my king;
When I shall voice aloud how good
   He is, how great should be,
Enlargèd winds that curl the flood
   Know no such liberty.

Stone walls do not a prison make,
   Nor iron bars a cage;
Minds, innocent and quiet, take
   That for a hermitage:
If I have freedom in my love,
   And in my soul am free; –
Angels alone, that soar above,
   Enjoy such liberty.

Cards and Kisses

Cupid and my Campaspe play'd
At cards for kisses – Cupid paid:
He stakes his quiver, bow, and arrows,
His mother's doves, and team of sparrows;
Loses them too; then down he throws
The coral of his lips, the rose
Growing on's cheek (but none knows how);
With these, the crystal of his brow,
And then the dimple of his chin:
All these did my Campaspe win.
At last he set her both his eyes –
She won, and Cupid blind did rise.
   O Love! has she done this for thee?
   What shall, alas! become of me?

Tell Me My Heart If This Be Love

When Delia on the plain appears,
Awed by a thousand tender fears,
I would approach, but dare not move; –
Tell me, my heart, if this be love.

Whene'er she speaks, my ravished ear
No other voice than hers can hear,
No other wit but hers approve; –
Tell me, my heart, if this be love.

If she some other swain commend,
Though I was once his fondest friend,
His instant enemy I prove; –
Tell me, my heart, if this be love.

When she is absent, I no more
Delight in all that pleased before –
The clearest spring, the shadiest grove; –
Tell me, my heart, if this be love.

When, fond of power, of beauty vain,
Her nets she spread for every swain,
I strove to hate, but vainly strove; –
Tell me, my heart, if this be love.

Virginia (Lays of Ancient Rome)

(Extract)

Just then, as through one cloudless chink in a black stormy
   sky,
Shines out the dewy morning-star, a fair young girl came by.
With her small tablets in her hand, and her satchel on her
   arm,
Home she went bounding from the school, nor dreamed of
   shame or harm;
And past those dreaded axes she innocently ran,
With bright, frank brow that had not learned to blush at
   gaze of man;
And up the Sacred Street she turned, and, as she danced
   along,
She warbled gaily to herself lines of the good old song,
How for a sport the princes came spurring from the camp,
And found Lucrece, combing the fleece, under the midnight
   lamp.
The maiden sang as sings the lark, when up he darts his
   flight,
From his nest in the green April corn, to meet the morning
   light;
And Appius heard her sweet young voice, and saw her sweet
   young face,
And loved her with the accursed love of his accursed race,
And all along the Forum, and up the Sacred Street,
His vulture eye pursued the trip of those small glancing feet.

Praise of Women

No thyng is to man so dere
As wommanys love in gode manere.
A gode womman is mannys blys,
There here love right and stedfast is.
There is no solas under hevene,
Of alle that a man may nevene,
That shuld a man do so moche glew
As a gode womman that loveth trew.
Ne derer is none in Goddys hurde
Than a chaste womman with lovely worde.

The Passionate Shepherd to His Love

Come live with me and be my love,
And we will all the pleasures prove
That valleys, groves, hills and fields,
Or woods or steepy mountain yields.

And we will sit upon the rocks,
And see the shepherds feed their flocks
By shallow rivers, to whose falls
Melodious birds sing madrigals.

And I will make thee beds of roses
And a thousand fragant posies;
A cap of flowers, and a kirtle
Embroidered all with leaves of myrtle.

A gown made of the finest wool
Which from our pretty lambs we pull;
Fair linèd slippers for the cold,
With buckles of the purest gold.

A belt of straw and ivy-buds
With coral clasps and amber studs:
And if these pleasures may thee move,
Come live with me and be my love.

Thy shepherd swains shall dance and sing
For thy delight each May morning:
If these delights thy mind may move,
Then live with me and be my love.

An Epitaph

Enough; and leave the rest to Fame!
'Tis to commend her, but to name.
Courtship which, living, she declined,
When dead, to offer were unkind:
Nor can the truest wit, or friend,
Without detracting, her commend.

To say – she lived a virgin chaste
In this age loose and all unlaced;
Nor was, when vice is so allowed,
Of virtue or ashamed or proud;
That her soul was on Heaven so bent,
No minute but it came and went;
That, ready her last debt to pay,
She summ'd her life up every day;
Modest as morn, as mid-day bright,
Gentle as evening, cool as night:
– 'Tis true; but all too weakly said.
'Twas more significant, she's dead.

Love's Grave

Mark where the pressing wind shoots javelin-like,
Its skeleton shadow on the broad-back'd wave!
Here is a fitting spot to dig Love's grave;
Here where the ponderous breakers plunge and strike,
And dart their hissing tongues high up the sand:
In hearing of the ocean, and in sight
Of those ribb'd wind-streaks running into white.
If I the death of Love had deeply plann'd,

I never could have made it half so sure,
As by the unblest kisses which upbraid
The full-waked sense; or failing that, degrade!
'Tis morning: but no morning can restore
What we have forfeited. I see no sin:
The wrong is mix'd. In tragic life, God wot,
No villain need be! Passions spin the plot:
We are betray'd by what is false within.

Did Not

'Twas a new feeling – something more
Than we had dared to own before,
    Which then we hid not;
We saw it in each other's eye,
And wished, in every half-breathed sigh,
    To speak, but did not.

She felt my lips' impassioned touch –
'Twas the first time I dared so much,
    And yet she chid not;
But whispered o'er my burning brow,
'Oh, do you doubt I love you now?'
    Sweet soul! I did not.

Warmly I felt her bosom thrill,
I pressed it closer, closer still,
   Though gently bid not;
Till – oh! the world hath seldom heard
Of lovers, who so nearly erred,
   And yet, who did not.

'Love is enough...'

Love is enough: though the World be a-waning,
And the woods have no voice but the voice of complaining,
    Though the sky be too dark for dim eyes to discover
The gold-cups and daisies fair blooming thereunder,
Though the hills be held shadows, and the sea a dark wonder
    And this day draw a veil over all deeds pass'd over,
Yet their hands shall not tremble, their feet shall not falter;
The void shall not weary, the fear shall not alter
    These lips and these eyes of the loved and the lover.

My Dream

Here is a dream.
It is my dream,
My own dream,
I dreamt it.
I dreamt that my hair was kempt,
Then I dreamt that my true love unkempt it.

'I do not love thee...'

I do not love thee! – no! I do not love thee!
And yet when thou art absent I am sad;
    And envy even the bright blue sky above thee,
Whose quiet stars may see thee and be glad.

I do not love thee! – yet, I know not why,
Whate'er thou dost seems still well done, to me:
    And often in my solitude I sigh
That those I do love are not more like thee!

I do not love thee! – yet, when thou art gone,
I hate the sound (though those who speak be dear)
    Which breaks the lingering echo of the tone
Thy voice of music leaves upon my ear.

I do not love thee! – yet thy speaking eyes,
With their deep, bright, and most expressive blue,
    Between me and the midnight heaven arise,
Oftener than any eyes I ever knew.

I know I do not love thee! yet, alas!
Others will scarcely trust my candid heart;
    And oft I catch them smiling as they pass,
Because they see me gazing where thou art.

The Enchantment

I did but look and love awhile,
    'Twas but for one half-hour;
Then to resist I had no will,
    And now I have no power.

To sigh and wish is all my ease;
    Sighs which do heat impart
Enough to melt the coldest ice,
    Yet cannot warm your heart.

O would your pity give my heart
    One corner of your breast,
'Twould learn of yours the winning art,
    And quickly steal the rest.

'Ca' the yowes to the knowes'

Ca' the yowes to the knowes,
Ca' them where the heather grows,
Ca' them where the burnie rows,
   My bonnie dearie.

As I gaed down the water side,
There I met my shepherd lad;
He row'd me sweetly in his plaid,
   And he ca'd me his dearie.

'Will ye gang down the water side,
And see the waves sae sweetly glide
Beneath the hazels spreading wide?
   The moon it shines fu' clearly.'

'I was bred up at nae sic school,
My shepherd lad, to play the fool,
And a' the day to sit in dool,
   And naebody to see me.'

'Ye sall get gowns and ribbons meet,
Cauf-leather shoon upon your feet,
And in my arms ye'se lie and sleep,
    And ye sall be my dearie.'

'If ye'll but stand to what ye've said,
I'se gang wi' you, my shepherd lad,
And ye may row me in your plaid,
    And I sall be your dearie.'

'While waters wimple to the sea,
While day blinks in the lift sae hie,
Till clay-cauld dath sall blin' my e'e,
    Ye aye sall be my dearie!'

Song

When thy beauty appears
In its graces and airs
All bright as an angel new dropp'd from the sky,
At distance I gaze and am awed by my fears:
So strangely you dazzle my eye!

But when without art
Your kind thoughts you impart,
When your love runs in blushes through every vein;
When it darts from your eyes, when it pants in your heart,
Then I know you're a woman again.

There's a passion and pride
In our sex (she replied),
And thus, might I gratify both, I would do:
Still an angel appear to each lover beside,
But still be a woman to you.

The Married Lover

Why, having won her, do I woo?
  Because her spirit's vestal grace
Provokes me always to pursue,
  But, spirit-like, eludes embrace;
Because her womanhood is such
  That, as on court-days subjects kiss
The Queen's hand, yet so near a touch
  Affirms no mean familiarness;
Nay, rather marks more fair the height
  Which can with safety so neglect
To dread, as lower ladies might,
  That grace could meet with disrespect;
Thus she with happy favour feeds
  Allegiance from a love so high
That thence no false conceit proceeds
  Of difference bridged, or state put by;

Because although in act and word
     As lowly as a wife can be,
Her manners, when they call me lord,
     Remind me 'tis by courtesy;
Not with her least consent of will,
     Which would my proud affection hurt,
But by the noble style that still
     Imputes an unattain'd desert;
Because her gay and lofty brows,
     When all is won which hope can ask,
Reflect a light of hopeless snows,
     That bright in virgin ether bask;
Because, though free of the outer court
     I am, this Temple keeps its shrine
Sacred to Heaven; because, in short,
     She's not and never can be mine.

'Hot sun, cool fire, temper'd with sweet air'

Hot sun, cool fire, temper'd with sweet air,
Black shade, fair nurse, shadow my white hair,
Shine, sun, burn, fire, breathe air and ease me,
Black shade, fair nurse, shroud me and please me;
Shadow (my sweet nurse) keep me from burning,
Make not my glad cause, cause of mourning.
      Let not my beauty's fire
      Enflame unstaid desire,
      Nor pierce any bright eye
      That wand'reth lightly.

The Apparition

My dead Love came to me, and said:
　'God gives me one hour's rest
To spend upon the earth with thee:
　How shall we spend it best?'

'Why, as of old,' I said, and so
　We quarrell'd as of old.
But when I turn'd to make my peace
　That one short hour was told.

To Helen

Helen, thy beauty is to me
   Like those Nicèan barks of yore
That gently, o'er a perfumed sea,
   The weary way-worn wanderer bore
   To his own native shore.

On desperate seas long wont to roam,
   Thy hyacinth hair, thy classic face,
Thy Naiad airs have brought me home
   To the glory that was Greece,
And the grandeur that was Rome.

Lo, in yon brilliant window-niche
   How statue-like I see thee stand,
   The agate lamp within thy hand,
Ah! Psyche, from the regions which
   Are holy land!

The Rape of the Lock

(Extract)

This nymph, to the destruction of mankind,
Nourished two locks, which graceful hung behind
In equal curls, and well conspired to deck
With shining ringlets the smooth ivory neck.
Love in these labyrinths his slaves detains,
And mighty hearts are held in slender chains.
With hairy springes we the birds betray,
Slight lines of hair surprise the finny prey,
Fair tresses man's imperial race ensnare,
And beauty draws us with a single hair.
    Th' advent'rous Baron the bright locks admired;
He saw, he wish'd, and to the prize aspired.
Resolved to win, he meditates the way,
By force to ravish, or by fraud betray;
For when success a lover's toil attends,
Few ask if fraud or force attain'd his ends.

Her Reply

If all the world and love were young,
And truth in every shepherd's tongue,
These pretty pleasures might me move
To live with thee and be thy Love.

But Time drives flocks from field to fold;
When rivers rage and rocks grow cold;
And Philomel becometh dumb;
The rest complains of cares to come.

The flowers do fade, and wanton fields
To wayward Winter reckoning yields:
A honey tongue, a heart of gall,
Is fancy's spring, but sorrow's fall.

Thy gowns, thy shoes, thy beds of roses,
Thy cap, thy kirtle, and thy posies,
Soon break, soon wither – soon forgotten,
In folly ripe, in reason rotten.

Thy belt of straw and ivy-buds,
Thy coral clasps and amber studs, –
All these in me no means can move
To come to thee and be thy Love.

But could youth last, and love still breed,
Had joys no date, nor age no need,
Then these delights my mind might move
To live with thee and be thy Love.

The Milkmaid's Epithalamium

Joy to the bridegroom and the bride
That lie by one another's side!
O fie upon the virgin beds,
No loss is gain but maidenheads.
Love quickly send the time may be
When I shall deal my rosemary!

I long to simper at a feast,
To dance, and kiss, and do the rest.
When I shall wed, and bedded be
O then the qualm comes over me,
And tells the sweetness of a theme
That I ne'er knew but in a dream.

You ladies have the blessed nights,
I pine in hope of such delights.
And silly damsel only can
Milk the cows' teats and think on man:
And sigh and wish to taste and prove
The wholesome sillabub of love.

Make haste, at once twin-brothers bear;
And leave new matter for a star.
Women and ships are never shown
So fair as when their sails be blown.
Then when the midwife hears your moan,
I'll sigh for grief that I have none.

And you, dear knight, whose every kiss
Reaps the full crop of Cupid's bliss,
Now you have found, confess and tell
That single sheets do make up hell.
And then so charitable be
To get a man to pity me.

Grown and Flown

I loved my love – alas to see
That this should be, alas!
I thought that this could scarcely be,
Yet has it come to pass:
Sweet sweet love was,
Now bitter bitter grown to me.

I loved my love from green of Spring
Until sere Autumn's fall;
But now that leaves are withering
How should one love at all?
One heart's too small
For hunger, cold, love, everything.

I loved my love on sunny days
Until late Summer's wane;
But now that frost begins to glaze
How should one love again?
Nay, love and pain
Walk wide apart in diverse ways.

A Death-Parting

Leaves and rain and the days of the year,
    (Water-willow and wellaway,)
All these fall, and my soul gives ear,
And she is hence who once was here.
    (With a wind blown night and day.)

Ah! but now, for a secret sign,
    (The willow's wan and the water white,)
In the held breath of the day's decline
Her very face seemed pressed to mine.
    (With a wind blown day and night.)

O love, of my death my life is fain;
    (The willows wave on the water-way,)
Your cheek and mine are cold in the rain,
But warm they'll be when we meet again.
    (With a wind blown night and day.)

Mists are heaved and cover the sky;
    (The willows wail in the waning light,)
O loose your lips, leave space for a sigh, –
They seal my soul, I cannot die.
    (With a wind blown day and night.)

DANTE GABRIEL ROSSETTI

Leaves and rain and the days of the year,
   (Water-willow and wellaway,)
All still fall, and I still give ear,
And she is hence, and I am here.
   (With a wind blown night and day.)

Dorinda

Dorinda's sparkling wit, and eyes,
    Uniting cast too fierce a light,
Which blazes high, but quickly dies,
    Pains not the heart, but hurts the sight.

Love is a calmer, gentler joy,
    Smooth are his looks and soft his pace,
Her Cupid is a black-guard boy
    That runs his link full in your face.

The Rover's Adieu

A weary lot is thine, fair maid,
    A weary lot is thine!
To pull the thorn thy brow to braid,
    And press the rue for wine.
A lightsome eye, a soldier's mien,
    A feather of the blue,
A doublet of the Lincoln green –
    No more of me ye knew,
        My Love!
No more of me ye knew.

'This morn is merry June, I trow,
    The rose is budding fain;
But she shall bloom in winter snow
    Ere we two meet again.'
– He turn'd his charger as he spake
    Upon the river shore,
He gave the bridle-reins a shake,
    Said 'Adieu for evermore,
        My Love!
And adieu for evermore.'

To Cloris

Cloris, I cannot say your eyes
Did my unwary heart surprise;
Nor will I swear it was your face,
Your shape, or any nameless grace:
For you are so entirely fair,
To love a part, injustice were;
No drowning man can know which drop
Of water his last breath did stop;
So when the stars in heaven appear,
And join to make the night look clear;
The light we no one's bounty call,
But the obliging gift of all.
He that does lips or hands adore;
Deserves them only, and no more;
But I love all, and every part,
And nothing less can ease my heart.
Cupid, that lover, weakly strikes,
Who can express what 'tis he likes.

Venus and Adonis

(*Extract*)

Sometime she shakes her Head, and then his Hand;
Now gazeth she on him, now on the Ground;
Sometime her Arms enfold him like a Band.
She would, he will not in her Arms be bound;
     And when from thence he struggles to be gone,
     She locks her Lily Fingers one in one.

'Fondling,' she saith, 'Since I have hemm'd thee here
Within the Circuit of this Iv'ry Pale,
I'll be a Park, and thou shalt be my Deer.
Feed where thou wilt, on Mountain or in Dale;
     Graze on my Lips, and if those hills be dry
     Stray lower, where the pleasant Fountains lie.

'Within this Limit is Relief enough,
Sweet Bottom Grass, and high delightful Plain,
Round rising Hillocks, Brakes obscure and rough,
To shelter thee from Tempest and from Rain.
     Then be my Deer, since I am such a Park;
     No Dog shall rouse thee, though a thousand bark.'

The Reconcilement

Come, let us now resolve at last
    To live and love in quiet;
We'll tie the knot so very fast
    That Time shall ne'er untie it.

The truest joys they seldom prove
    Who free from quarrels live:
'Tis the most tender part of love
    Each other to forgive.

When least I seem'd concern'd, I took
  No pleasure nor no rest;
And when I feign'd an angry look,
  Alas! I loved you best.

Own but the same to me – you'll find
  How blest will be our fate.
O to be happy – to be kind –
  Sure never is too late!

Love's Philosophy

The fountains mingle with the river,
   And the rivers with the ocean,
The winds of heaven mix for ever
   With a sweet emotion;
Nothing in the world is single;
   All things by a law divine
In one another's being mingle –
   Why not I with thine?

See, the mountains kiss high heaven,
   And the waves clasp one another;
No sister flower would be forgiven
   If it disdained its brother:
And the sunlight clasps the earth,
   And the moonbeams kiss the sea –
What are all these kissings worth
   If thou kiss not me?

To Mistress Margery Wentworth

With margerain gentle,
  The flower of goodlihead,
Embroidered the mantle
  Is of your maidenhead.
Plainly I cannot glose;
  Ye be, as I divine,
The pretty primrose,
  The goodly columbine.

Benign, courteous, and meek,
  With wordes well devised;
In you, who list to seek,
  Be virtues well comprised.
With margerain gentle,
  The flower of goodlihead,
Embroidered the mantle
  Is of your maidenhead.

I Remember

It was my bridal night I remember,
An old man of seventy-three
I lay with my young bride in my arms,
A girl with t.b.
It was wartime, and overhead
The Germans were making a particularly heavy raid on
    Hampstead.
Harry, do they ever collide?
I do not think it has ever happened,
Oh my bride, my bride.

Love Cannot Die

They sin who tell that love can die:
With life all other passions fly,
All others are but vanity.
In heaven ambition cannot dwell,
Nor avarice in the vaults of hell:
Earthly these passions, as of earth,
They perish where they have their birth.
  But Love is indestructible;
Its holy flame for ever burneth,
From heaven it came, to heaven returneth.
Too oft on earth a troubled guest,
At times deceived, at times opprest;
  It here is tried and purified,
And hath in heaven its perfect rest;
It soweth here with toil and care,
But the harvest-time of love is there.
Oh! when a mother meets on high
The babe she lost in infancy,
Hath she not then for pains and fears,
  The day of woe, the anxious night,
For all her sorrow, all her tears,
  An over-payment of delight?

Romance

I will make you brooches and toys for your delight
Of bird-song at morning and star-shine at night.
I will make a palace fit for you and me,
Of green days in forests and blue days at sea.

I will make my kitchen, and you shall keep your room,
Where white flows the river and bright blows the broom,
And you shall wash your linen and keep your body white
In rainfall at morning and dewfall at night.

And this shall be for music when no one else is near,
The fine song for singing, the rare song to hear!
That only I remember, that only you admire,
Of the broad road that stretches and the roadside fire.

Chloris in the Snow

I saw fair Chloris walk alone,
When feather'd rain came softly down,
As Jove descending from his Tower
To court her in a silver shower:

The wanton snow flew to her breast,
Like pretty birds into their nest,
But, overcome with whiteness there,
For grief it thaw'd into a tear:
      Thence falling on her garments' hem,
      To deck her, froze into a gem.

The Constant Lover

Out upon it, I have loved
    Three whole days together!
And am like to love three more,
    If it prove fair weather.

Time shall moult away his wings
    Ere he shall discover
In the whole wide world again
    Such a constant lover.

But the spite on 't is, no praise
    Is due at all to me:
Love with me had made no stays,
    Had it any been but she.

Had it any been but she,
    And that very face,
There had been at least ere this
    A dozen dozen in her place.

The Lute and the Lyre

Deep desire, that pierces heart and spirit to the root,
Finds reluctant voice in verse that yearns like soaring fire,
Takes exultant voice when music holds in high pursuit
    Deep desire.

Keen as burns the passion of the rose whose buds respire,
Strong as grows the yearning of the blossom toward the fruit,
Sounds the secret half unspoken ere the deep tones tire.

Slow subsides the rapture that possessed love's flower-soft lute,
Slow the palpitation of the triumph of the lyre:
Still the soul feels burn, a flame unslaked though these be mute.
    Deep desire.

Marriage Morning

Light, so low upon earth,
    You send a flash to the sun.
Here is the golden close of love,
    All my wooing is done.
Oh, the woods and the meadows,
    Woods where we hid from the wet,
Stiles where we stay'd to be kind,
    Meadows in which we met!

Light, so low in the vale
    You flash and lighten afar,
For this is the golden morning of love,
    And you are his morning star.
Flash, I am coming, I come,
    By meadow and stile and wood,
Oh, lighten into my eyes and heart,
    Into my heart and my blood!

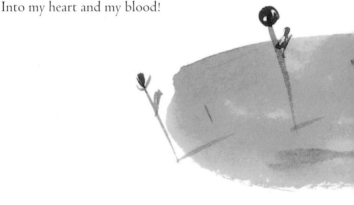

Heart, are you great enough
    For a love that never tires?
O heart, are you great enough for love?
    I have heard of thorns and briers.
Over the thorns and briers,
    Over the meadows and stiles,
Over the world to the end of it
    Flash for a million miles.

Sorrows of Werther

Werther had a love for Charlotte
    Such as words could never utter;
Would you know how first he met her?
    She was cutting bread and butter.

Charlotte was a married lady,
    And a moral man was Werther,
And, for all the wealth of Indies,
    Would do nothing for to hurt her.

So he sighed and pined and ogled,
    And his passion boiled and bubbled,
Till he blew his silly brains out,
    And no more was by it troubled.

Charlotte, having seen his body
    Borne before her on a shutter,
Like a well-conducted person,
    Went on cutting bread and butter.

Love in the Asylum

A stranger has come
To share my room in the house not right in the head,
A girl mad as birds

Bolting the night of the door with her arm her plume.
Strait in the mazed bed
She deludes the heaven-proof house with entering clouds

Yet she deludes with walking the nightmarish room,
At large as the dead,
Or rides the imagined oceans of the male wards.

She has come possessed
Who admits the delusive light through the bouncing wall,
Possessed by the skies

She sleeps in the narrow trough yet she walks the dust
Yet raves at her will
On the madhouse boards worn thin by my walking tears.

And taken by light in her arms at long and dear last
I may without fail
Suffer the first vision that set fire to the stars.

Gifts

Give a man a horse he can ride,
  Give a man a boat he can sail;
And his rank and wealth, his strength and health,
  On sea nor shore shall fail.

Give a man a pipe he can smoke,
  Give a man a book he can read:
And his home is bright with a calm delight,
  Though the room be poor indeed.

Give a man a girl he can love,
  As I, O my love, love thee;
And his heart is great with the pulse of Fate,
  At home, on land, on sea.

Rivals

Of all the torments, all the cares,
    With which our lives are curst;
Of all the plagues a lover bears,
    Sure rivals are the worst!
By partners in each other kind
    Afflictions easier grow;
In love alone we hate to find
    Companions of our woe.

Sylvia, for all the pangs you see
    Are labouring in my breast,
I beg not you would favour me,
    Would you but slight the rest!
How great soe'er your rigours are,
    With them alone I'll cope;
I can endure my own despair,
    But not another's hope.

The Imprisoned Soul

At the last, tenderly,
From the walls of the powerful, fortress'd house,
From the clasp of the knitted locks – from the keep of the
   well-closed doors,
Let me be wafted.

Let me glide noiselessly forth;
With the key of softness unlock the locks – with a whisper
Set ope the doors, O soul!

A Song of a Young Lady to Her Ancient Lover

Ancient person, for whom I
All the flattering youth defy,
Long be it ere thou grow old,
Aching, shaking, crazy, cold;
    But still continue as thou art,
    Ancient person of my heart.

On thy withered lips and dry,
Which like barren furrows lie,
Brooding kisses I will pour
Shall thy youthful heat restore
(Such kind showers in autumn fall,
And a second spring recall);
    Nor from thee will ever part,
    Ancient person of my heart.

The nobler part, which but to name
In our sex would be counted shame,
By age's frozen grasp possessed,
From his ice shall be released,
And soothed by my reviving hand,
In former warmth and vigour stand.
All a lover's wish can reach
For thy joy my love shall teach,
And for thy pleasure shall improve
All that art can add to love.
 Yet still I love thee without art,
 Ancient person of my heart.

'She dwelt among the untrodden ways'

She dwelt among the untrodden ways
    Beside the springs of Dove,
A Maid whom there were none to praise
    And very few to love:

A violet by a mossy stone
    Half hidden from the eye!
Fair as a star, when only one
    Is shining in the sky.

She lived unknown, and few could know
    When Lucy ceased to be;
But she is in her grave, and, oh,
    The difference to me!

'Quondam was I in my lady's grace'

Quondam was I in my lady's grace,
I think as well as now be you;
And when that you have trad the trace,
Then shall you know my words be true,
    That quondam was I.

Quondam was I. She said for ever:
That lasted but a short while;
Promise made not to dissever.
I thought she laugh'd – she did but smile,
    Then quondam was I.

Quondam was I: he that full oft lay
In her arms with kisses many one.
It is enough that this I may say,
Though among the moo now I be gone,
    Yet quondam was I.

Quondam was I. Yet she will you tell
That since the hour she was first born
She never loved none half so well
As you. But what altho she had sworn,
    Sure quondam was I.

When You are Old

When you are old and grey and full of sleep,
And nodding by the fire, take down this book,
And slowly read, and dream of the soft look
Your eyes had once, and of their shadows deep;

How many loved your moments of glad grace,
And loved your beauty with love false or true,
But one man loved the pilgrim soul in you,
And loved the sorrows of your changing face;

And bending down beside the glowing bars,
Murmur, a little sadly, how Love fled
And paced upon the mountains overhead
And hid his face amid a crowd of stars.

~ Index of titles or first lines

~ Acknowledgements

The editor and publisher wish to thank the following for permission to use copyright material:

John Betjeman, for 'In a Bath Teashop' from *Collected Poems* by John Betjeman, by permission of John Murray (Publishers) Ltd; E. E. Cummings, for 'i like my body when it is with your body...' from *Complete Poems 1904–1962* by E. E. Cummings, edited by George J. Firmage. Copyright © 1991 by the Trustees for the E. E. Cummings Trust and George James Firmage, by permission of W. W. Norton & Company; Emily Dickinson, for 'My life closed twice before its close' from *The Poems of Emily Dickinson*, edited by Thomas H. Johnson, The Belknap Press of Harvard University Press. Copyright © 1951, 1955, 1979 by the President and Fellows of Harvard College, by permission of Harvard University Press and the Trustees of Amherst College; Robert Graves, for 'Down, Wanton, Down!' from *Complete Poems* by Robert Graves, by permission of Carcanet Press; Seamus Heaney, for 'A Dream of Jealousy' from *Field Work* by Seamus Heaney, Faber & Faber and *Opened Ground: Selected Poems 1966–1996* by Seamus Heaney, Farrar, Straus & Giroux. Copyright © 1998 by Seamus Heaney, by permission of Faber & Faber Ltd and Farrar, Straus & Giroux LLC; A. E. Housman, for 'When I was one-and-twenty...', by permission of The Society of Authors as the Literary Representative of the Estate of the author; Philip Larkin, 'Annus Mirabilis' from *High Windows*, Faber & Faber and *Collected Poems* by Philip Larkin, Farrar, Straus & Giroux, by permisison of Faber & Faber Ltd and Farrar, Straus & Giroux LLC; Ogden Nash, for